MOTHER TERESA

MOTHER TERESA

ODYSSEYS

LAURA K. MURRAY

CREATIVE EDUCATION · CREATIVE PAPERBACKS

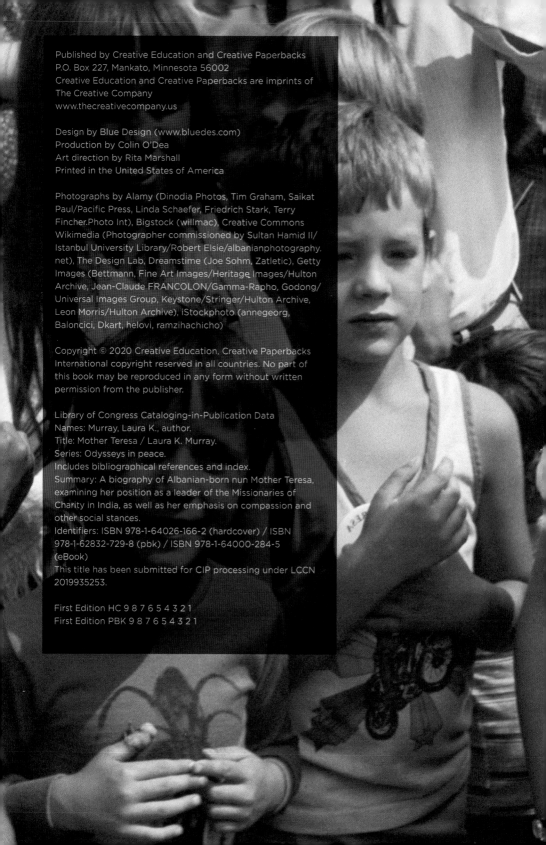

Published by Creative Education and Creative Paperbacks
P.O. Box 227, Mankato, Minnesota 56002
Creative Education and Creative Paperbacks are imprints of
The Creative Company
www.thecreativecompany.us

Design by Blue Design (www.bluedes.com)
Production by Colin O'Dea
Art direction by Rita Marshall
Printed in the United States of America

Photographs by Alamy (Dinodia Photos, Tim Graham, Saikat
Paul/Pacific Press, Linda Schaefer, Friedrich Stark, Terry
Fincher.Photo Int), Bigstock (willmac), Creative Commons
Wikimedia (Photographer commissioned by Sultan Hamid II/
Istanbul University Library/Robert Elsie/albanianphotography.
net), The Design Lab, Dreamstime (Joe Sohm, Zatletic), Getty
Images (Bettmann, Fine Art Images/Heritage Images/Hulton
Archive, Jean-Claude FRANCOLON/Gamma-Rapho, Godong/
Universal Images Group, Keystone/Stringer/Hulton Archive,
Leon Morris/Hulton Archive), iStockphoto (annegeorg,
Baloncici, Dkart, helovi, ramzihachicho)

Library of Congress Cataloging-in-Publication Data
Names: Murray, Laura K., author.
Title: Mother Teresa / Laura K. Murray.
Series: Odysseys in peace.
Includes bibliographical references and index.
Summary: A biography of Albanian-born nun Mother Teresa,
examining her position as a leader of the Missionaries of
Charity in India, as well as her emphasis on compassion and
other social stances.
Identifiers: ISBN 978-1-64026-166-2 (hardcover) / ISBN
978-1-62832-729-8 (pbk) / ISBN 978-1-64000-284-5
(eBook)
This title has been submitted for CIP processing under LCCN
2019935253.

First Edition HC 9 8 7 6 5 4 3 2 1
First Edition PBK 9 8 7 6 5 4 3 2 1

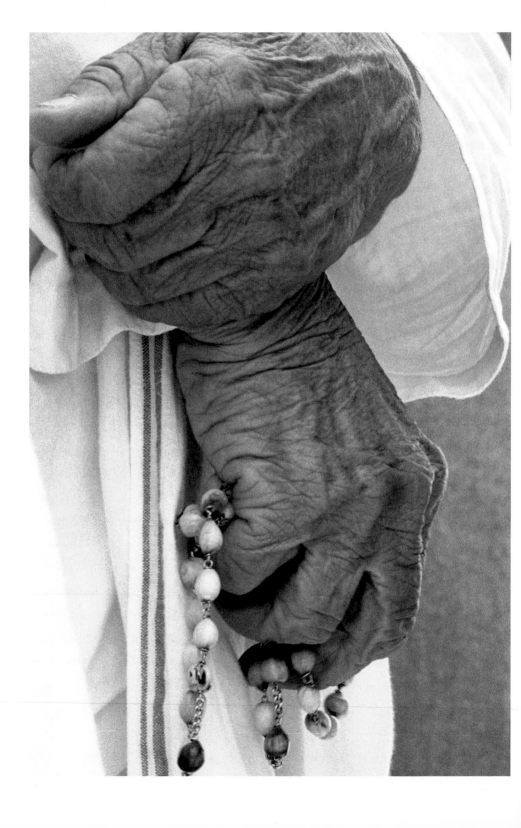

CONTENTS

Introduction

The small, elderly nun presented a striking image, whether she was walking through filthy streets, laying her hands on the sick and dying, or petitioning foreign leaders and leading orphans out of war zones. Wherever she went, she offered fervent prayers for peace and encouraged joy amidst suffering.

The world knew Mother Teresa as one of the greatest humanitarians in recent history. By the time of her

OPPOSITE: Mother Teresa left home at the age of 18 and spent the rest of her life away from her family as she served the poor and suffering in India.

death in 1997, she had captured the hearts of millions. Her religious order comprised thousands of members and spanned the globe. Not everyone agreed she was worthy of praise, though. Criticisms of her work and motivations continued throughout her life and after her death. Neither her critics nor her supporters knew that she had experienced a spiritual struggle for decades.

Known at various times as "the Saint of the Gutters" and eventually "Saint Teresa of Calcutta" in the Catholic Church, Mother Teresa lived according to the principle of loving simply. Her faith compelled her to do the difficult work of caring for society's unwanted and forgotten. Doing so, she believed, would bring light into the world. The unassuming nun clad in white and blue had known since childhood that she was meant to serve others. She could not have predicted that she would eventually become an international symbol of peace.

Call to India

The little girl who would become known as Mother Teresa was born Anjezë (Agnes) Bojaxhiu on August 26, 1910. Agnes grew up in Skopje, the present-day capital of the Republic of Macedonia. At that time, Skopje was part of Yugoslavia in the Ottoman Empire. Agnes was the youngest of three children in a Catholic Albanian family. She was often called Gonxha, Albanian for "flower bud."

Agnes's father, Nikola, was a

OPPOSITE: At the time of Agnes's birth, Skopje was called Üsküp; the region experienced several changes in leadership during her lifetime.

successful contractor involved in politics. Her mother, Dranafile, was especially devout, taking the children to Mass and delivering food to the poor. The family lived in a large home, and Agnes's parents taught their children to help others in need. Being both Catholic and of Albanian descent, the family was a minority in Skopje. The church offered them a sense of belonging to a community.

When Agnes was eight years old, her father died unexpectedly. Afterward, the family was left with little. Still, they continued helping others in need. Dranafile provided strangers with food, clothing, and kindness. She started a successful business selling embroidery and cloth to support the family.

Catholicism played a prominent role in the family's everyday life. Agnes was heavily involved in her local parish. The church offered not only religious but also social activities for young Agnes, who enjoyed playing the mandolin and having picnics with friends. She also taught religion to younger children. Even at the age of 12, Agnes felt God was calling her to be a missionary. Her mother's selfless giving helped inspire Agnes's own desire to serve others. A Jesuit priest named Father Franio Jambrenkovic was also influential. He led Agnes's parish youth group and shared exciting stories about missionary work in other lands.

As Agnes got older, she prayed about her future. Devoting her life to religious work would be difficult. She would have to leave her family. Unsure of what to do, she discussed the matter with Father Jambrenkovic. He advised that if she felt happy at the idea of a certain life, it was a sign of the right path. "Joy that comes from the depths of your being is like a compass by which you can tell what direction your life should follow," he said. "That is the case, even when the road you must take is a difficult one."

Agnes decided she was willing to go wherever God called her. In 1928, at age 18, Agnes left home to be a missionary. Dranafile told her daughter, "Put your hand in [Jesus's] hand, and walk alone with Him. Walk ahead, because if you look back, you will go back." Agnes and her mother would not see each other again.

Alone, Agnes sailed to Dublin, Ireland. She joined the religious community of the Institute of the Blessed Virgin Mary. Known as the Sisters of Loreto, these nuns focused on education. They had missions and schools in India and other places around the world. Agnes took the name Sister Mary Teresa, after French-born Saint Thérèse of

Quenching the Thirst

The phrase "I thirst" was central to Mother Teresa's philosophy. According to the Bible, Jesus spoke the words before dying on the cross. They have been interpreted as not only a literal cry for water but also a symbolic one for people to accept Jesus into their hearts. Through prayer and acts of service, Missionaries of Charity is dedicated to quenching that thirst. According to biographer Navin Chawla, Mother Teresa thought the phrase also referenced Christ living within the poor, whom Mother Teresa was devoted to serving.

Lisieux (1873–97). Like her patron saint Thérèse, Agnes believed that doing small, simple actions with love could lead to holiness.

S ister Teresa was assigned to a Loreto community in Calcutta, India (now known as Kolkata). She arrived there in early 1929. She was sent to the West Bengal town of Darjeeling to complete her novitiate, the two-year period of training and prayer before becoming a nun. In May 1931, Sister Teresa made her first vows to become a nun. Afterward, she was assigned to teach at a Loreto

UBLIN

SKOPJE

DARJEELING

KOLKATA

INDIAN OCEAN

TAKEAWAY

"Don't look for big things, just do small things with great love…. The smaller the thing, the greater must be our love."

high school for girls in Kolkata called St. Mary's. Sister Teresa made her final vows in 1937. From then on, she was called Mother Teresa.

Mother Teresa was overjoyed to dedicate her life as a nun. She often referred to herself as Jesus's "little spouse." She believed that if she sacrificed and suffered in her own life, she would be closer to Jesus, who had suffered by being crucified. Her fellow Sisters of Loreto became like family to her. She also loved teaching history and geography at St. Mary's and later became its principal. Students and fellow sisters knew her for her kindness, cheerfulness, humility, and joy in hard work. "Don't look for big things, just do small things with great love…. The smaller the thing, the greater must be our love," she said. She would remain at St. Mary's until 1948.

Mother Teresa was deeply affected by the poverty she encountered outside her convent and school. Each week, Mother Teresa went into the overcrowded, impoverished areas known as slums to visit the poor and sick. One of her early visits was to a family afflicted by poverty and tuberculosis. Although she thought it was painful to witness their hardship and not be able to offer them material comfort, Mother Teresa could tell the visit encouraged the family. The mother asked Mother Teresa to come again, saying, "Your smile brought sun into this house!" Mother Teresa prayed that she would be strong enough to be a hopeful presence in their lives and accomplish her goal of teaching them about God.

Mother Teresa's students and fellow sisters admired

War and Famine

In 1942, the British Army took over Mother Teresa's school of St. Mary's, using it as a military hospital. Nuns and students who boarded at the school were evacuated to a nearby city. They returned to Kolkata a few months later and remained in rented space for the next four years. Then the region experienced a major famine in 1943. In 1946, the year before India gained independence from Great Britain, bloody riots between Hindus and Muslims erupted in Kolkata. Mother Teresa left the convent to find food and was stopped by soldiers: "I told them I had to come out and take the risk; I had 300 students who had nothing to eat." The soldiers drove her back to the school and gave her bags of rice.

her work with the poor. However, they did not know about a secret vow she had taken. In addition to her public vows to become a nun, in 1942, she had privately committed to doing everything for Jesus, not refusing him anything. This vow was not revealed until after her death. According to biographer Father Brian Kolodiejchuk, the private vow laid the foundation for all of Mother Teresa's actions and future work. It meant she would obey Jesus's call blindly, even when it was difficult or she did not fully understand. Mother Teresa's commitment to taking and honoring vows was rooted in her Albanian background. Kolodiejchuk explains that, in Albanian culture, someone's word of honor carries much weight; it cannot be broken, even at risk of death.

In 1946, the course of Mother Teresa's life changed. In September, the 36-year-old reportedly had an encounter with Jesus in what would become known as her "Inspiration Day." Jesus told her to leave Loreto and serve the marginalized, the lonely, and the poorest of the poor. According to Mother Teresa, he said, "Come, be my light." She referred to his command as her "second calling." She would later relate hearing Jesus's direct voice and having visions on various occasions.

Soon Mother Teresa came to a decision: she would leave her beloved school and convent. She would devote all her energy to attending to the poor and suffering. But her path forward was not yet clear. She later remembered, "I was to leave the convent and work with the poor, living among them. It was an order. I knew where I belonged, but I did not know how to get there."

"From the age of 5½ years,—when I first received [**Holy Communion**]—the love for souls has been within—It grew with the years—until I came to India—with the hope of saving many souls."

- Letter from Mother Tereesa to **Archbishop** Ferdinand Périer, 1947

A New Mission Begins

Following her new calling to serve the poorest of the poor proved challenging. Although she was anguished at the thought of leaving behind her life as a Loreto nun, she would do it, because she believed that was what Jesus asked of her. But she faced a bigger hurdle. As a nun, she had taken a vow of obedience. Before she could move ahead with her calling, she needed official permission from

OPPOSITE: Slums are neighborhoods of makeshift housing in which homes, often made from pieces of metal and trash, lack basic services, such as running water and heat.

the Catholic Church.

She wrote letters to her superiors, telling them that Jesus's voice had told her to start a religious order called the Missionaries of Charity. She explained that the sisters' lives would be based in poverty to bring souls to God. She reported that Jesus had told her to start schools and hospitals and to care for the sick and dying. He told her to live like the poor and to dress "simple and poor" in an Indian sari that would become a holy symbol.

Mother Teresa's superiors were unwilling to approve her request immediately. Although Archbishop Ferdinand Périer never doubted her sincerity, he needed time to decide. He wanted to make sure that her own self-interest was not guiding her request, among other considerations. Mother Teresa was distraught at having to wait. She continued to write to the archbishop over the next two

In 1947, India gained independence from Britain. The country's movement for independence had lasted 90 years.

years, outlining her plan in more detail as he asked for specifics. "It is for you to use me, to offer me to God for the poor," she wrote. "I feel sometimes afraid, for I have nothing, no brains, no learning, no qualities required for such a work, and yet I tell [Jesus] that my heart is free from everything and so it belongs completely to Him."

As Mother Teresa looked to embark on her new journey, India was entering a new stage of history. In 1947, the country gained independence from Britain. India's movement for independence had lasted 90 years, gaining steam after World War II. Kolkata was a key center during the movement. After independence, the population of India grew as refugees flowed into the city.

This caused slums to grow as well. Mother Teresa was increasingly eager to devote her life to the poor.

n January 1948, Archbishop Périer granted Mother Teresa permission to move forward. She next had to gain approvals from higher-ranking church officials. Finally, in August 1948, Pope Pius XII gave Mother Teresa permission to leave the Loreto community and follow her calling. Her aim would be to care for the dying and vulnerable. Through simple acts, she would give them dignity and compassion and teach them about God.

After a short training in basic medicine, Mother

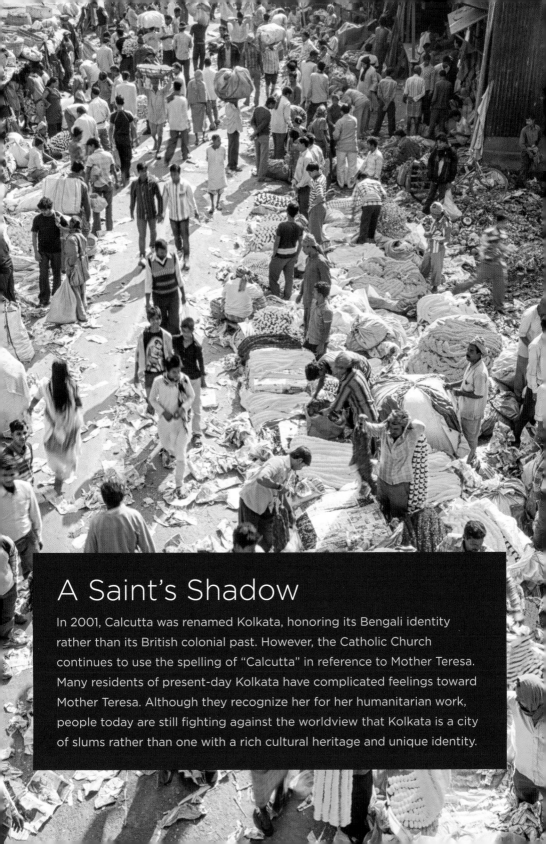

A Saint's Shadow

In 2001, Calcutta was renamed Kolkata, honoring its Bengali identity rather than its British colonial past. However, the Catholic Church continues to use the spelling of "Calcutta" in reference to Mother Teresa. Many residents of present-day Kolkata have complicated feelings toward Mother Teresa. Although they recognize her for her humanitarian work, people today are still fighting against the worldview that Kolkata is a city of slums rather than one with a rich cultural heritage and unique identity.

In joining the Missionaries of Charity, nuns took a vow "to give wholehearted, free service to the very poorest."

Teresa went out into the streets and homes of Kolkata. Small in stature, she wore sandals and the white-and-blue cotton sari for which she would become known. She carried a rosary. She walked for miles. Sometimes she had to beg for supplies so that she could give out food, water, and medicine. She washed people's sores and brought them to hospitals. Volunteers soon joined her, including former students from St. Mary's. They established a small, open-air school for children.

Despite working tirelessly among the poor and sick, Mother Teresa encouraged others to remain cheerful. She often talked about spreading love through small deeds. According to her, Jesus's suffering was not unlike the suffering of the poor. Donations began to arrive, aiding the organization's growth. In 1950, Mother Teresa became an Indian citizen.

B y then, Mother Teresa's community had grown to 12 people. In October, the archbishop officially established the Society of the Missionaries of Charity in the Archdiocese of Calcutta. Mother Teresa would become known throughout the world for her work in this order. In joining the Missionaries of Charity, nuns took a vow "to give wholehearted, free service to the very poorest."

Studying the Effects

Mother Teresa's international renown has made her the subject of scientific studies as well. For example, in 2014, a study published in the *International Journal of Emergency Health* examined how stress management and spirituality affected compassion fatigue or burnout of mental health workers. The researchers concluded that spirituality may help in preventing compassion fatigue and may increase compassion satisfaction among professional caregivers. They called these findings the "Mother Teresa effect." The same year, Texas researchers published their study on the effects of charities using celebrities or famous humanitarians to promote their cause. They titled their study "The Mother Teresa Effect."

Like Mother Teresa, the sisters wore white-and-blue habits. In Mother Teresa's view, they had to experience poverty themselves and should reject wealth.

In 1952, Missionaries of Charity, now at 26 members, opened a free hospice in an abandoned Hindu temple donated by the Indian government. Called Nirmal Hriday ("home of the pure heart"), the home took in the dying to offer them comfort, basic care, and dignity. When hospitals refused to accept people as "hopeless cases," the sisters brought them to the hospice. A few years later, the Missionaries opened a children's home called Shishu Bhavan ("children's home of the immaculate heart"). Over the next decade, the Missionaries of Charity established leprosy centers, nursing homes, and orphanages throughout the country.

In 1965, Pope Paul VI named the Missionaries of

Charity an official International Religious Family. Missionaries of Charity continued to expand, forming new branches for both men and women in several countries. In 1971, the group opened its first home in the United States. By 1975, the order reportedly numbered more than 1,000 sisters in 15 countries.

While her community grew, Mother Teresa was facing a secret struggle. No one except a few advisers knew that she suffered from what she called "the darkness." Around the time she began serving the poor, she began feeling a spiritual hopelessness and longing that continued for the rest of her life. She felt rejected and abandoned by the God to whom she was devoting her life. These hidden internal struggles were in stark contrast to her public attitude of joyful service. She once wrote to an adviser: "I am told God lives in me—and yet the reality

of darkness and coldness and emptiness is so great that nothing touches my soul." These experiences would not surface publicly until after her death.

Still, Mother Teresa was unceasing in her work. She received numerous awards for promoting peace, including the Pope John Paul XXIII Peace Prize and the John F. Kennedy International Award, both in 1971. In 1979, she received the Nobel Peace Prize. The committee highlighted her work to address poverty as a means to promoting peace. According to the announcement, "Constructive efforts to do away with hunger and poverty, and to ensure for mankind a safer and better world community in which to develop, should be inspired by the spirit of Mother Teresa, by respect for the worth and dignity of the individual human being."

While accepting the prize in Oslo, Norway, Mother

Teresa wore her signature sari and led the ceremony attendees in a prayer for peace by Saint Francis of Assisi. She related a story of an impoverished woman who shared the little she received with neighbors in need. She added, "If I stay here the whole day and the whole night, you would be surprised of the beautiful things that people do, to share the joy of giving." A portion of Mother Teresa's speech notably focused on her anti-abortion stance.

The world was taking notice of the unassuming little nun. As Mother Teresa's fame and public admiration soared, critics appeared. They began to more closely examine the work and motivations of the woman who was often referred to as a "living saint."

"In these 20 years of work among the people, I have come more and more to realize that it is being unwanted that is the worst disease that any human being can ever experience."

- Mother Teresa, Nobel Peace Prize acceptance speech, 1979

The World at Attention

Throughout the 1980s and 1990s, Mother Teresa captured international attention. Startling television footage showed the little nun making her way through the streets of India, attending to the sick and poor. To many viewers, she represented a way of living simply and offering help to those in need. This was especially powerful to those who felt the world was becoming too focused on material wealth. But to

OPPOSITE: Mother Teresa gained worldwide fame for her work and during her life met with several world leaders, including U.S. presidents Ronald Reagan, George H. W. Bush, and Bill Clinton.

45

While the media portrayed Kolkata as a dirty, miserable place filled with death, disease, and suffering, it presented Mother Teresa as a white savior.

some, it seemed the world was being misled about Mother Teresa's work and motivations. Critics voiced their concerns while Mother Teresa was alive, and examinations have continued into the present day.

One of Mother Teresa's main critics was British Indian author and physician Aroup Chatterjee. In 2002, he published a book describing what he saw as misconceptions and falsehoods about Mother Teresa. In what he refers to as "the Teresa Myth," Chatterjee asserts that the international media promoted a misleading image of Mother Teresa as a saintly figure. While the media portrayed Kolkata as a dirty, miserable place filled with death, disease, and suffering, it presented Mother Teresa as a white savior. Chatterjee writes that these depictions are Western stereotypes.

Criticism of Mother Teresa and Missionaries of Charity centered on the conditions of their facilities. Despite the donations pouring in, little was done to equip the centers or to ensure basic comfort and care for those who sought refuge there. Some volunteers reported being shocked at the homes' lack of basic medical equipment and the workers' lack of simple medical knowledge.

Introducing Mother Teresa

British journalist Malcolm Muggeridge (pictured) is often credited with introducing Mother Teresa to the world. His 1968 BBC interview with Mother Teresa drew a positive response for the network, with audiences entranced by the small nun's good deeds. Donations promptly began to flow in to Missionaries of Charity. Next, Muggeridge made a 1969 documentary on Mother Teresa called *Something Beautiful for God*. He wrote a book by the same name in 1971. Later, critics would accuse Muggeridge of contributing to a misleading narrative of Mother Teresa's work and of falsely claiming a miracle during filming.

TAKEAWAY

British author Christopher Hitchens, one of Mother Teresa's sharpest critics, pointed out that the Missionaries of Charity glorified suffering.

Volunteer Mary Loudon recalled that needles were reused without being sterilized and that hospice patients received no basic pain medication. According to another volunteer, "Prayer is their method, their technology." The homes did not separate those with treatable illnesses from those with untreatable ones. Workers were also accused of secretly performing baptisms for dying patients without their consent. In various homes, child patients were not allowed to have any stimulation or entertainment. The issue, some said, was that the Missionaries' goal was saving souls rather than addressing medical needs.

British author Christopher Hitchens, one of Mother

Teresa's sharpest critics, pointed out that the Missionaries of Charity glorified suffering. He contested that much of the questionable treatment stemmed from the order's belief that pain and suffering were gifts that allowed a person to share in Jesus's pain. Mother Teresa's defenders argued that the Missionaries were doing their best to care for the forgotten and dying and to help bring them to God. How could critics fault the order for devoting their lives to helping those whom no one else was helping?

In 1980, the Missionaries of Charity opened homes for people suffering from drug addiction and women who had been abused. A few years later, they opened a hospice for people with AIDS in New York. But critics questioned not only what they saw as the Missionaries' regressive social views but also their absence in various Indian relief efforts. For example, Chatterjee writes that

Kolkata's missionaries were nowhere to be found during regional tragedies such as a factory explosion that killed nearly two dozen child laborers or a fire that wiped out hundreds of slum dwellings.

Mother Teresa continued to receive awards for her work. In 1980, she received the Bharat Ratna (Jewel of India) award and, in 1985, the U.S. Presidential Medal of Freedom. As her fame grew, Mother Teresa became one of the most recognizable faces of the Catholic Church. The hardworking "saint

Siege of Beirut

Mother Teresa made headlines for her role in the 1982 Lebanon War. In August of that year, she joined relief workers to evacuate 37 children from a hospital near a refugee camp in Beirut, Lebanon. The children, many of whom had disabilities, had been left in squalid conditions. The hospital was in the line of fighting and had already experienced bombings. During a ceasefire, the group brought the children through the Palestinian and Israeli lines. The children were taken out of the war zone to a facility opened by Mother Teresa.

of the gutters" seemed to show that the Church could be a force for good. Mother Teresa met with politicians and business leaders from around the world—including Princess Diana and U.S. president Ronald Reagan—often at their request. During her travels, she advocated strongly against abortion and divorce.

In 1991, Mother Teresa wrote an open letter to U.S. president George H. W. Bush and Iraqi president Saddam Hussein. She asked them to avoid war. "Let love and peace triumph and let your names be remembered for the good you have done, the joy you have spread, and the love you have shared," she wrote. The letter did not change Bush's decision to start Operation Desert Storm a few weeks later.

Mother Teresa's relationships with controversial or violent political figures became points of contention.

Some people who donated to her cause were political leaders who suppressed human rights in their own countries but were seemingly sympathetic toward Mother Teresa. For example, she had a relationship with Haitian dictator Jean-Claude Duvalier. She was close to an American fraudster who donated generously and let her use his private jet. Robert Hanssen, a Russian double agent inside the FBI, was another donor. On the subject of her questionable donors, Mother Teresa told her biographer Navin Chawla, "We have no right to judge anybody. God alone has that right." To her, it was more important to fund the mission than to quibble with others. She would continue her work. Mother Teresa's fellow nuns tried to defend her by pointing out that Jesus's methods were also criticized.

During the 1980s and '90s, Mother Teresa's health

Mother Teresa died of heart failure in Kolkata on September 5, 1997. She was 87 years old. At that time, the Missionaries of Charity numbered more than 4,000.

began to fail. She accepted advanced medical treatment, such as a pacemaker and heart surgery, while her own facilities continued to be criticized for lack of basic medical care. Despite her health issues, people close to her reported that she radiated her trademark joy and humility. She kept traveling around the world, attending the openings of new facilities and meeting with world leaders. The fall of communism allowed her to bring her messages to Central and Eastern Europe. In 1996, she received honorary U.S. citizenship.

Mother Teresa died of heart failure in Kolkata on

September 5, 1997. She was 87 years old. At that time, the Missionaries of Charity numbered more than 4,000. Thousands of mourners attended her state funeral, as well as foreign dignitaries such as Queen Sofia of Spain, Queen Noor of Jordan, and American First Lady Hillary Rodham Clinton. "Her goodness was contagious," said Archbishop Henry D'Souza. "It invited others to share."

Mother Teresa was buried at the Missionaries of Charity's Mother House in Kolkata. Believers immediately began making pilgrimages to her tomb. With public opinion sky-high, Mother Teresa would soon be on the fast track to sainthood.

"Crossing the frontiers of religious and ethnic differences, she has taught the world this lesson: It is more blessed to give than to receive."

- Cardinal Angelo Sodano at Mother Teresa's funeral, 1997

Legacy of a Saint

A person must undergo an official evaluation process to be canonized, or declared a saint, in the Catholic Church. The process includes the documentation of testimonies, interviews, and votes by church officials. As a rule, the process cannot begin until five years after death. This ensures the person's public popularity is not the reason for her consideration. In Mother Teresa's case, Pope John Paul II waived part of the waiting

OPPOSITE: Today, thousands of volunteers work with Missionaries of Charity houses all over the world, including 244 in India alone.

period and began the process in 1999.

In order to be a saint, two miracles attributed to the person must be approved—one for beatification and one for canonization. The first of Mother Teresa's miracles was the 1998 healing of an Indian woman's abdominal tumor. After a medal that had touched Mother Teresa was placed on the woman's stomach, the tumor disappeared. This miracle was disputed by both the woman's doctor and her husband, as the woman had undergone other medical treatment that could have accounted for the result. The second miracle was the 2008 full recovery of a Brazilian man with a severe brain infection. He had prayed to Mother Teresa for help and had a relic of her placed on his head.

In October 2003, Mother Teresa was beatified by the pope. "Mother Teresa, an icon of the Good Samaritan, went everywhere to serve Christ in the poorest of the poor," he said. "Not even conflict and war could stand in her way." Beatification was the last step before sainthood. Her fervent supporters included not only Catholics but also many Hindus and Muslims. During the process, two of her harshest critics, Christopher Hitchens and Aroup Chatterjee, both offered evidence to the Church against declaring her a saint.

Mother Teresa's inner faith struggles surfaced during the beatification process. In 2007, her personal letters were made public in a book called *Mother Teresa: Come Be My Light*. The book was edited by Canadian priest Brian Kolodiejchuk, who led Mother Teresa's beatification and canonization. Much of the world was shocked to learn of the nun's spiritual turmoil. Mother Teresa had never wanted the letters to be read and had requested

Anything but a Saint?

A controversial 2013 study by University of Montreal researchers found that Mother Teresa was "anything but a saint." The researchers cited common criticisms, including her "rather dubious" medical care and her "suspicious management of the enormous sums of money she received." They suggested that the Catholic Church had quickly declared her a saint to harness good public relations. However, the researchers added that she likely inspired other people who have made positive differences in the lives of those in need.

"She would be able to share that empathy because she herself was experiencing it…. For me, this darkness is the single most heroic aspect of her life."

her advisers to destroy them. Kolodiejchuk and church leaders attested that Mother Teresa's feelings of darkness made her a holy person who shared in the suffering of Jesus and the poor whom she served. "She understood very well when people would share their horror stories, their pain and suffering of being unloved, lonely," Kolodiejchuk said. "She would be able to share that empathy because she herself was experiencing it…. For me, this darkness is the single most heroic aspect of her life."

On September 4, 2016, Mother Teresa was canonized as Saint Teresa of Calcutta by Pope Francis. He declared her a saint before cheering crowds in St. Peter's Square in Vatican City. Francis added that the world would still go on calling her Mother Teresa as they knew her. Only one other person in modern history—Pope John Paul II in 2014—had attained sainthood faster.

Mother Teresa left a mixed legacy. She is widely admired for her calls for peace as well as for her work in caring for the poor, demonstrating that everyone is worthy of dignity. Still, ongoing debates surround the portrayal of her larger-than-life role in India in general and Kolkata in particular. Missionaries of Charity, some

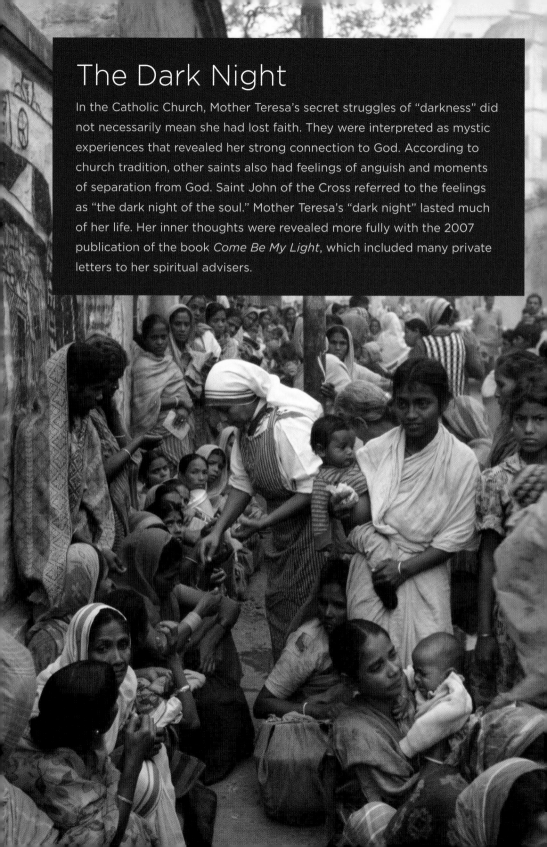

The Dark Night

In the Catholic Church, Mother Teresa's secret struggles of "darkness" did not necessarily mean she had lost faith. They were interpreted as mystic experiences that revealed her strong connection to God. According to church tradition, other saints also had feelings of anguish and moments of separation from God. Saint John of the Cross referred to the feelings as "the dark night of the soul." Mother Teresa's "dark night" lasted much of her life. Her inner thoughts were revealed more fully with the 2007 publication of the book *Come Be My Light*, which included many private letters to her spiritual advisers.

say, has had a minimal impact on helping Kolkata's poor. They assert that other charitable organizations have taken a much more active role in helping those in need. "Did she ever open a single good school in Calcutta, or a first-rate hospital?" questioned Indian politician Saugata Roy. "Did she ever work to help the victims of drought or floods in West Bengal?... The Jesuits [who run schools in Calcutta] have done more." Other critics focus on lasting negative stereotypes of India throughout the rest of the world.

The order that Mother Teresa felt called to establish in 1946 now stretches far and wide. According to its website, the Missionaries of Charity has grown to include more than 5,000 sisters serving in 758 houses in 139 countries. It encompasses branches of male religious members as well. Several foundations have been established in Mother Teresa's name, including those that offer free medical clinics and educational scholarships.

Missionaries of Charity has continued to be known for its conservative views and adherence to traditional church practices. In 2015, the order made international headlines when it shut down its adoption services in India. This was in response to India's new adoption rules that allowed adoptions by single, separated, and divorced people. "Our rules only allow married couples to adopt," the head sister of one Missionaries home told the American news service National Public Radio. This attitude was met with criticism because of the large number of orphans in India needing homes.

In 2018, the Indian government began investigating Missionaries of Charity after a nun and an employee were arrested on charges of selling babies for adoption.

Authorities in one region canceled the licenses of seven of the organization's children's homes after their investigation found various problems, from expired licenses to overcrowding.

Mother Teresa's tomb at Kolkata's Missionaries of Charity Mother House is considered a religious shrine, or holy place dedicated to her. Pilgrims can visit a small museum and Mother Teresa's room. They can also see other places associated with Mother Teresa and the Missionaries of Charity. The order's official website, motherteresa.org, lists the addresses of a hospice, leprosy center, church, and other sites. It includes information on places Mother Teresa lived and worked, such as St. Mary's High School.

Despite ongoing criticisms, Mother Teresa has remained an icon of peace in modern times. To various groups, she is remembered as a zealot, a myth, a humanitarian, a figurehead, and a saint. Throughout her life, she demonstrated that one person can draw the world's attention to the plight of those most in need. Her way was simple: to love the unloved and forgotten. Her story continues to inspire millions to show love through small deeds, even when it is difficult. Her focus on serving the poor ignited a following of dedicated missionaries and volunteers that spans the globe. Millions of people from many faiths and backgrounds continue to heed her call to be lights in the darkness.

"By blood, I am Albanian. By citizenship, an Indian. By faith, I am a Catholic nun. As to my calling, I belong to the world. As to my heart, I belong entirely to the heart of Jesus."

— **Mother Teresa**

Timeline

1910   Anjezë (Agnes) Gonxha Bojaxhiu is born in Skopje, in present-day Macedonia, on August 26.

1928   Agnes leaves home to become a missionary with the Sisters of Loreto. She arrives in Dublin, Ireland, and takes the name Sister Mary Teresa.

1929   Sister Teresa arrives in Calcutta (Kolkata), India, on January 6.

1937   Sister Teresa takes her final vows as a nun. She is known as Mother Teresa.

1942   Mother Teresa takes a private vow to obey anything Jesus asks of her.

1946   On September 10, Mother Teresa receives her "second calling" to serve the poorest of the poor.

1947   India gains independence from Great Britain on August 15.

1948   Mother Teresa leaves the Sisters of Loreto to follow her new calling.

1950   Archbishop Ferdinand Périer officially establishes Mother Teresa's order, the Missionaries of Charity, in the Archdiocese of Calcutta.

1979   Mother Teresa accepts the Nobel Peace Prize on December 10, amid growing fame and criticism.

1997   Mother Teresa dies in Kolkata at age 87 on September 5.

2003   On October 19, Pope John Paul II beatifies Mother Teresa.

2007 Many of Mother Teresa's private letters are published in the book *Mother Teresa: Come Be My Light*, revealing her inner struggles more fully than ever before.

2016 On September 4, Pope Francis declares Mother Teresa a saint in the Catholic Church.

Selected Bibliography

Chatterjee, Aroup. *Mother Teresa: The Untold Story.* New Delhi: Fingerprint, 2016.

Chawla, Navin. *Mother Teresa: The Authorized Biography.* Boston: Element Books, 1996.

John Paul II. "Beatification of Mother Theresa of Calcutta: Homily of His Holiness John Paul II." Libreria Editrice Vaticana. 2003. *http://w2.vatican.va/content/john-paul-ii /it/homilies/2003/documents/hf_jp-ii_hom_20031019_ mother-theresa.html.*

Kolodiejchuk, Brian, ed. *Mother Teresa: Come Be My Light: The Private Writings of the "Saint of Calcutta."* New York: Doubleday, 2007.

Mother Teresa of Calcutta Center. *Mother Teresa Center.* http:// www.motherteresa.org.

Norwegian Nobel Institute "Mother Teresa Facts." *Nobel Peace Prize.* https://www.nobelprize.org/nobel_prizes/peace /laureates/1979/.

Sebba, Anne. "Chapter 1: Origins." *Mother Teresa: Beyond the Image."* New York Times on the Web, 1997. https://archive .nytimes.com/www.nytimes.com/books/first/s/sebba -teresa.html?mcubz=1.

Wilbur, Charles K. "Mother Teresa." *The SAGE Encyclopedia of World Poverty*. Ed. Mehmet Odekon. 2nd ed. Thousand Oaks, Calif.: SAGE, 2015. DOI: 10.4135/9781483345727.n565.

Endnotes

abortion	the ending of a human pregnancy before an embryo or fetus can survive on its own; the medical procedure of deliberate abortion is distinguished from natural abortion (such as miscarriages or stillbirths); traditional Catholic teaching is morally opposed to deliberate abortion
archbishop	a Catholic bishop who is in charge of an area's churches (known as an archdiocese)
baptisms	religious ceremonies that are outward signs of individuals' entrance into the Christian Church and their belonging to the family of God
beatification	being declared by a pope to be blessed after death
communism	a system of government in which all property and business is owned and controlled by the state, with the goal of creating a classless society
convent	a Catholic community for nuns
crucified	put to death by nailing to a cross
dictator	a ruler with complete power

Holy Communion	in the Catholic Church, a holy rite involving bread and wine that is the most important act of worship; Catholics believe that the bread and wine become the body and blood of Jesus Christ
hospice	a place that provides care for people with long-standing or incurable illnesses
Jesuit	a member of the Society of Jesus, a Roman Catholic order of priests
leprosy	a contagious disease that affects the skin
minority	a group that differs from the larger group, or majority
missionary	a person who travels to another place to promote religion
Operation Desert Storm	a 1991 military operation led by the U.S. to remove Iraqi forces from Kuwait during the Gulf War
patron saint	a guiding saint that gives special prayers and protection
pilgrimages	journeys made to a holy place
relic	physical remains or a personal possession of a saint
rosary	a string of beads meant for keeping count of prayers
sari	a draping garment traditionally worn by women in India and other places in South Asia

stereotypes	general beliefs about a group of people
tuberculosis	an infectious disease usually affecting the lungs
vows	public promises committing to the lifestyle and behaviors of a religious community

Websites

Nobel Peace Prize 1979
https://www.nobelprize.org/nobel_prizes/peace/laureates/1979/

Read more about Mother Teresa's life and the Nobel Peace Prize.

Saint Teresa of Calcutta: Her Words
https://www.ewtn.com/motherteresa/herwords.asp

Learn more about Mother Teresa's canonization and philosophies.

Note: Every effort has been made to ensure that any websites listed above were active at the time of publication. However, because of the nature of the Internet, it is impossible to guarantee that these sites will remain active indefinitely or that their contents will not be altered.

Index